Contents

Life processes in animals and plants

Living and non-living things

Plants, animals and human beings are all living things. There are many differences between living things and those things that have never been alive. For example, a tortoise looks very similar to a stone, but a tortoise can walk and breathe and is alive. In contrast a stone cannot do these things since it is not a living thing.

Life processes

All living things have several things in common. From **fungi** to fish, from broad beans to butterflies, from tigers to tall trees, living things all carry out the same actions. There are seven of these activities and they are known as life processes.

You can tell if something is alive if it does all of these things:

- It needs food to survive. We call this **nutrition**.
- It gets rid of waste. We call this **excretion**.
- It can move part or all of itself. We call this movement.
- It gets bigger over time. We call this growth.
- It uses **oxygen** to get **energy** from food. We call this **respiration**.
- It produces offspring. We call this **reproduction**.
- It reacts to changes in its **environment**. We call this **sensitivity**.

For something to be alive it must do *all* these things. Some non-living things may seem to do some of these things but they do not do all of them. For instance, a river is full of *moving* water, but it is not alive. A sand dune may *grow* bigger as more sand is deposited, but it is not alive. An iceberg melts as the sea and air around it get warmer, but it is not alive.

These seven life processes are necessary for any living thing to stay alive.

LIF   ES

AND   GS

Heinemann
LIBRARY

www.heinemann.co.uk/library

Visit our website to find out more information about **Heinemann Library** books.

To order:

 Phone 44 (0) 1865 888066

 Send a fax to 44 (0) 1865 314091

Visit the Heinemann Bookshop at www.heinemann.co.uk/library to browse our catalogue and order online.

First published in Great Britain by Heinemann Library, Halley Court, Jordan Hill, Oxford OX2 8EJ, part of Harcourt Education. Heinemann is a registered trademark of Harcourt Education Ltd.

© Harcourt Education Ltd 2002
The moral right of the proprietor has been asserted.

Produced for Heinemann Library by Discovery Books Ltd
Editorial: Nick Hunter and Jennifer Tubbs
Design: Ian Winton
Production: Viv Hichens
Picture research: Maria Joannou

Originated by Ambassador Litho Ltd
Printed in Hong Kong, China by
Wing King Tong

ISBN 0 431 17440 7 (hardback)
06 05 04 03 02
10 9 8 7 6 5 4 3 2 1

ISBN 0 431 17444 X (paperback)
07 06 05 04 03
10 9 8 7 6 5 4 3 2 1

British Library Cataloguing in Publication Data
Hunter, Rebecca
   Life Processes and living things. - (Explore Science)
   570
A full catalogue record for this book is available from the British Library.

Acknowledgements
The publishers would like to thank the following for permission to reproduce photographs:
Ardea: page **13**; Chris Honeywell: page **25** (bottom); Corbis: page **15**; Digital Vision: page **5** (bottom); FLPA: page **35** (top); Getty Images: page **26** (bottom); Nature Picture Library: page **40**; Oxford Scientific Films: pages **5** (mid), **5** (top), **6**, **8**, **11**, **17**, **18**, **20**, **22**, **23**, **25** (top), **28**, **30**, **31**, **32**, **33**, **34**, **35** (bottom), **36**, **37**, **38**, **39**, **41**, **42**; Photodisc: page **19**; Roger Scruton: page **16**; Science Photo Library: pages **9**, **10**, **12**, **14**, **27**, **29**, **43**, **44**; Trevor Clifford: page **7**; Wildlife matters: page **21**.

Cover photograph of fish reproduced with permission of Science Photo Library.

The publishers would like to thank Angela Royston for her contributions to the text of this book.

Every effort has been made to contact copyright holders of any material reproduced in this book. Any omissions will be rectified in subsequent printings if notice is given to the publishers.

Any words appearing in the text in **bold**, like this, are explained in the glossary.

Reproduction: All living things reproduce. This chick has just hatched from its egg.

Sensitivity: Plants will react to their environment. This tiny plant inside the broad bean seed has started to grow. It will grow upwards, towards the light.

Nutrition: All animals need food. One of a squirrel's favourite foods is nuts.

Exploring further

The Heinemann Explore CD-ROM will give you information on what humans and animals need to live. From the Contents screen, click on Exploring to find out more.

Nutrition

All animals need to eat. Just like cars need fuel to make them work, animals need food. Food is the body's fuel. It gives animals the **energy** to move, breathe, think and even sleep. Every part of an animal's body needs energy.

Most of the food you eat gives you energy. But it is important to eat a balanced diet to keep your body healthy.

Different animals have different diets. Some animals, like dogs and cats, eat mainly meat. Cows and sheep eat grass. This hamster eats vegetables and seeds.

Food

A balanced diet contains a variety of foods.
- **Starches**, sugar and **fats** give you energy. Bread, pasta, rice and potatoes are starchy foods. Sweets, cakes, biscuits, chocolate bars and sweet drinks all have a lot of sugar. Butter, oil, crisps, chips and sausages contain a large amount of fat.
- **Protein** helps you to grow. Meat, fish, cheese, beans and lentils all contain a lot of protein.
- **Vitamins** and **minerals** help you to grow well and stay healthy. Fruit, vegetables, milk, beans and fish all contain vitamins and minerals.
- **Fibre** helps your body to get rid of waste food. Fruit, vegetables, beans and wholemeal bread are full of fibre.

What vitamins and minerals do I need to stay healthy?

Your body needs vitamins and minerals to stay healthy. There are several kinds of vitamins.
- Vitamin A helps the body to fight disease and is found in carrots, fish and sweetcorn.
- Vitamin B is needed by **cells** so they can grow and function properly. Eggs, wholemeal bread and meat are rich in vitamin B.
- Vitamin C keeps skin healthy. It is found in raw fruit and vegetables.
- Vitamin D helps your bones to grow properly. There is a lot of vitamin D found in fish.

Two of the minerals your body needs are calcium and iron. Calcium in milk and cheese makes your bones and teeth strong. Your body needs iron to absorb **oxygen** properly.

There are many ways to eat a balanced diet. People from different countries and cultures often like certain kinds of food cooked in special ways. Vegetarians do not eat meat. They eat beans or cheese to give them protein.

Fruit and vegetables contain fibre. They also contain many different vitamins and minerals. You should eat five portions of fruit or vegetables each day.

Exploring further – Teeth and eating

You can find out more about the function of teeth in eating on the CD-ROM.
Follow this path: Contents > Digging Deeper > Eating and Digestion

Movement

Almost everything you do involves movement. You need to move, not only to get about, but to eat, get dressed, read a book, work and play. Moving means using your muscles and joints to move your bones.

Bones

Without bones you would be floppy and shapeless, like a jellyfish stranded on a beach. Bones give you your shape, but bones cannot bend. If you had only one bone in each leg and arm, you would move very stiffly. You can bend and move your body because you have many bones. All the bones in your body together are called the skeleton. Some animals have skeletons inside their bodies called internal skeletons. These animals are called **vertebrates**. Other animals have external (outside) skeletons.

These groups of animals have internal skeletons:
- **Mammals**: for example, humans, cats, mice and elephants.
- Birds: for example, chickens, pigeons and penguins.
- **Reptiles**: for example, snakes, dinosaurs and turtles.
- **Amphibians**: for example, frogs, newts and salamanders.
- Fish: for example, sharks, goldfish and tuna.

This picture shows how bones help to shape each animal. This skeleton belongs to a snake.

Joints

The places where bones meet are called joints. There are joints at your knees, elbows, ankles, wrists, fingers and toes. There are also many joints along your backbone which allow you to bend and twist. Joints are moved by muscles.

How do muscles work?

Muscle is the meaty substance that covers your bones. Your muscles are fixed to your bones by **tendons**. When a muscle tightens it becomes shorter. We call this contracting. As it contracts it pulls the tendon. The tendon pulls the bone it is fixed to. When the muscle relaxes, the pull stops. Muscles can pull but they cannot push, so most muscles work in pairs. When the muscle called the **biceps** in your upper arm contracts it pulls up your lower arm. To straighten your arm you have to contract the **triceps** muscle at the back of your upper arm.

This gymnast is using many muscles and joints to bend, stretch and move.

Exploring further – Muscles

The CD-ROM can show you how to find out more about how the muscles in the human body work. Follow this path: Exploring > Humans and other animals > Muscles and movement

Growth

All animals, including people, grow from a single **cell**. Some young animals hatch from an egg laid by the female. Human babies and many other animals develop inside the female and are born fully formed. Newly born animals are much smaller than their parents. They grow and develop until they are as big as their parents.

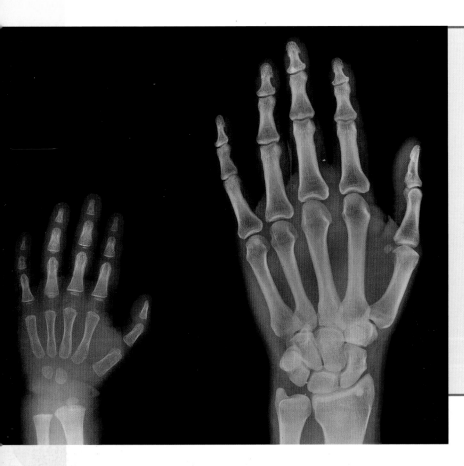

Bones grow longer and thicker. This is an X-ray. It shows a child's hand on the left and an adult's hand on the right. The ends of the child's bones are covered with **cartilage**. New bones grow from cartilage. Over a long time most cartilage changes into hard bone.

Wilhelm Röntgen,

Wilhelm Röntgen (1845–1923) discovered X-rays in 1895. X-rays can pass through skin, but not through bone. They create a picture of your bones.

X-rays have changed medicine and science. Doctors use them to study bones in living people and can now use them to study organs too. Scientists also use them. Röntgen was awarded a prize, called the Nobel Prize, for his achievement. He was the first person to be given the prize for physics.

Exoskeletons

Skeletons outside the body are called **exoskeletons**, or shells. Snails, crabs and shellfish have shells. They have no bones inside their bodies and as they grow, they build on to their shells at the lip. This is why shells are spiral in shape – they are continually being added to.

Insects and other **arthropods** also have a hard covering on the outside of their soft bodies. These hard plates do not grow as the animal inside grows. This means that as the animal grows, it has to shed its exoskeleton and grow a new, bigger one.

Some animals like worms and jellyfish have no hard skeleton either inside or outside their bodies. They have liquid in their bodies. This gives them their shape and protects their **organs**.

This desert scorpion has an outer shell or exoskeleton.

Exploring further – Bones and growing

You can discover more about animal skeletons on the CD-ROM. Follow this path: Contents > Quick Facts > Moving and Growing

Respiration

If you are to stay alive, your body **cells** need **energy**. Your cells release energy from food by a process known as **respiration**. For this to happen, **oxygen** is needed. Oxygen is a gas which is in the air all around us. Animals take in oxygen by breathing. You start to breathe the moment you are born and will carrying on breathing all the time, even when you are asleep, until you die.

Your breathing system begins in your nose (and mouth) and finishes in your lungs. Air enters the system through your nose or mouth and goes into the windpipe. This divides into smaller and smaller tubes in your lungs. Oxygen in the air passes through the thin lining of the lungs and into your blood. Red blood cells in the bloodstream then carry oxygen to all the cells in your body. The cells use it to burn food to create energy. Meanwhile, the rest of the air is breathed out, along with an unwanted gas called **carbon dioxide**, and **water vapour**.

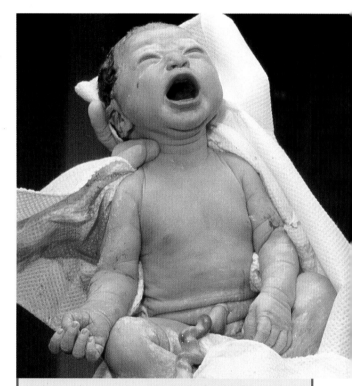

A baby girl takes her first breath. Before she was born the baby received the oxygen she needed from her mother's blood.

 How often do I breathe?

When sitting still, you breathe about 15 to 18 times a minute. Each breath is about 500 cubic centimetres of air (about the same as a small milk carton). If you run, you take deeper breaths more often. This means more oxygen goes into your blood to help produce the extra energy you need.

Two spotted dolphins swim to the surface to breathe in air.

Fish breathe by taking oxygen from water, not air. They have gills to help them do this. Water goes into the fish's mouth as it swims. The water flows over the gills, which take the oxygen out. Dolphins, however, are **mammals** and breathe just like we do. They swim to the surface and take in a gulp of air through their blowhole. Then, by closing their blowholes, dolphins can hold their breath to dive underwater. Some dolphins can hold their breath for up to 15 minutes, diving as deep as 200 metres!

Some insects breathe in air even though they live in water. They capture air in a bubble and then position the bubble near the openings to their breathing system. The great diving beetle stores air under its wings whilst underwater.

Exploring further – Human breathing

To find out more about how humans breathe, follow this path on the CD-ROM: Contents > Digging Deeper > Breathing

Reproduction

All around us new plants, insects and other animals are sprouting and growing. All kinds of living things must **reproduce** themselves if each kind is to survive. Every living thing has **organs** whose job is to create this new life.

Males and females

It takes a male and a female to make a new animal life. Males and females have different sexual organs. In humans, the man's sexual organs produce male sex **cells**, called sperm, and the woman's produce female sex cells, called eggs. A male sex cell must join with a female sex cell to make the first cell of a new animal. This first cell divides into more and more cells to form all the different kinds of cells in the body of the baby.

 How many cells are there in a human baby?

In humans it takes nine months for the growing baby to develop inside its mother. By the time the baby is ready to be born, the single cell has multiplied into 2000 million cells, making a new and completely separate human being!

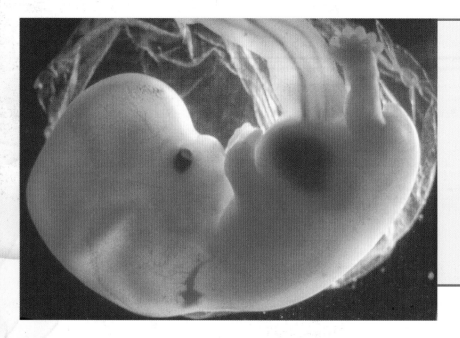

This is a human **embryo**. It is seven weeks old. The eyes are forming. The head is big compared to the body. The legs and arms are only tiny buds but the toes have already started to grow.

Animal babies

Some **mammal** babies, like lions and rabbits, are born blind and helpless. Other mammal babies, like antelope and horses, can see and run with their parents very soon after they are born.

Mammals must take care of their babies. Some build burrows or nests for them to live in. Mothers feed their babies milk from their **teats**. The milk is very rich and helps the babies grow quickly. Mammals need lots of food for **energy** and warmth. As the babies get older, their mothers gradually stop feeding them milk and the babies start eating solid food. The parents bring them food until they are old enough to find their own.

Baby birds also need a great deal of care from their parents. Birds build nests in which to lay their eggs. They protect the nests from enemies. If an enemy comes close to a place where birds are nesting, it may get attacked by the parents.

Parent birds bring food to the chicks until they are old enough to fly or leave the nest. Most chicks grow up very fast. Some are fully grown in only 20 days after hatching. Larger birds, however, may take up to a year to become adult.

These chicks cannot leave the nest immediately. The adult birds must feed them until they are ready to fly.

Exploring further – Human life cycle

The CD-ROM contains lots of information on the main stages of the human life cycle. Follow this path: Contents > Digging Deeper > Reproduction and Birth

Life cycles

In order to see how living things **reproduce** and grow, it is useful to look at their **life cycles**. A life cycle shows the whole course of development, from before birth to adulthood. Here we compare the life cycle of a bird with that of a **mammal**.

Life cycle of a chicken

A mother hen lays about twelve eggs. She sits on them to **incubate** them, or keep them warm. After four weeks the eggs hatch. The chick uses its beak to chip its way out of the shell. When it hatches, the little chick is wet but soon its feathers dry and become soft and fluffy.

The mother hen lays one egg a day for about twelve days. When the whole clutch is laid she starts sitting on them. She will barely leave the nest until they hatch.

As the chicks grow bigger their fluffy, yellow **down** is replaced by proper feathers. After two months the chicks are old enough to leave their mother. They can find their own food. They eat seeds, corn and worms.

At a year old, hens are ready to **mate**. The cockerel mates with the females to **fertilize** the eggs. The hen will then lay the eggs and in a month a new **brood** of chicks will hatch out.

Life cycle of a kangaroo

Kangaroos are **marsupial** mammals, which means the mothers rear their young in a pouch. A baby kangaroo is called a joey. The tiny new-born joey crawls through its mother's fur and into her pouch. There it finds a **teat** and holds on fast.

The joey spends six to eight months in the pouch. As it grows older, it looks out and nibbles at the grass as its mother feeds. Eventually the mother will tip it out of the pouch. When it is thirsty, the joey dips its head into its mother's pouch for a drink of milk. When it is tired, it can climb back in.

At 18 months old, the joey is too big to get into the pouch but it likes to stay quite close to its mother. Adult kangaroos and joeys stay together in a big group. They feed on grass and leaves.

The young joey still feeds on its mother's milk after it has left the pouch.

Young male kangaroos leave their mothers when they are between two and three years old. They are big enough to look after themselves and join a group of other young males. They will be old enough to mate at four years old.

Exploring further – Animal life cycles

Do you know the stages in the life cycles of a butterfly, mushroom or salmon? The CD-ROM contains information on these living things and many more. Follow this path: Contents > Digging Deeper > Animal life cycles.

Seeing and hearing

People and animals have senses to help them find out about the world.
They use their senses to see, hear, taste, smell and feel.

Seeing

People and many animals have two eyes which they use to see. Light enters
the eyes and meets the **retina** at the back of the eye. Special **cells** in the
retina send messages to the brain and the brain works out what is being
seen. The human eye is shaped like a ball. The eyeballs can move about so
that you can see things at the side as well as in front of you.

 How are animals eyes different to ours?

Animals' eyes are not always at the front of their head. Animals that
are eaten by other animals often have eyes at the sides of their heads.
This is so that they can look all around them for danger. Animals that
hunt usually have two eyes at the front of their head. Birds' eyes are
shaped like a long egg. This shape helps them to see far-away things
very clearly. Owls have eyes at the front of their heads and can turn
their heads all the way round so that they can see in all directions. The
chameleon can move each eye separately to look out for danger. Some
spiders have several pairs of eyes.

Flies have special
eyes that are
huge and made
of hundreds of
parts. They are
called compound
eyes and they
allow flies see all
around.

Hearing

You hear with your ears. You have two ears and they are on the sides of your head. Sounds are made when things vibrate. Different vibrations make loud sounds, soft sounds, high sounds and low sounds. You can hear most vibrations. The ear-drum inside the ear senses the vibrations and sends messages to the brain which tells you what the sounds are.

Most animals rely more on their sense of hearing than their sense of sight to catch food and avoid danger. The barn owl flies at night and listens very carefully. It can hear a mouse running in a field. Bats have a very well developed sense of hearing which they use to catch flying insects. Grasshoppers and crickets can hear sounds, but their ears are not on their heads – they are on their knees or the sides of their bodies!

Some animals use their ears to sense if their enemies are close by. The kangaroo rat has very good hearing. It lives in the desert and comes out at night. It can hear the tiny sound of the scales of a rattlesnake moving on the sand.

Hares have long ears to collect sound. Their good hearing often warns them of danger.

Exploring further – Senses in living things

Find out more about the senses of humans and animals on the CD-ROM.
Follow this path: Contents > Digging Deeper > Senses in living things

Tasting and smelling

Many animals use taste to find the foods they like. Giraffes like the new, tender leaves that grow on the trees in summer. These are full of **nutrients**, and are very good for the giraffes. **Mammals** taste things with their tongues. There are tiny lumps on the edges of your tongue and in your mouth called taste buds. When they taste something they send a message to your brain. The taste buds on different parts of the tongue sense different tastes: salt, like potato crisps; sweet, like chocolate; sour, like a lemon; or bitter, like the olives on a pizza. If you taste something nasty or that is not safe to eat, your brain tells you to spit it out quickly.

Most animals have **receptors** that taste their food. Sometimes they are very different to our tongues. A spider has special feelers called pedipalps to taste things. Lizards and snakes have a receptor in the roof of the mouth to smell and taste things. A snake waves its tongue and pushes the air onto the receptor so it can taste it.

A hummingbird likes to drink **nectar** from flowers.

Smelling

Smell is often the most important sense to an animal. They use it to find food and to avoid **predators**. Mammals smell with their noses. Noses can be all sorts of different shapes and sizes but they all work in the same way. When you breathe in air, any smells in the air go up your nose too. They touch special smell receptors inside your head. These tell your brain what you are smelling.

Most animals have some way of sensing smells around them. Many fish have nostrils at the front of their heads. They can smell scents in the water as they swim along. Insects like bees have feelers with smell receptors at the ends. Some flowers have strong scents. The feelers sense the smell, and guide the bees to the flowers.

Snails have two pairs of feelers. They stretch the short ones out in front as they move. They use them to smell what is around them.

Exploring further – Keeping healthy

Taste and smell are senses that help you to eat healthily. The CD-ROM contains other information about how to stay healthy. Follow this path: Exploring > Humans and other animals > Health and exercise

Touching

You feel with every part of your body, from the top of your head to the tips of your toes. Your skin is covered with **receptors** which recognize touching and feeling. **Nerves** send messages from the receptors to your brain when you touch something. If it hurts, your brain tells you to stop touching it.

Animals and touch

Touch is an important form of communication for animals. They often use parts of their bodies like humans use their hands. A mother elephant strokes her calf gently with her trunk to reassure it. A crocodile carries her babies to safety carefully in her mouth. Many animals use touch to groom each other. Monkeys stroke each other's fur to pick out mites. Some small fish clean bigger fish by picking **parasites** off with their lips.

Lion cubs spend much of their time touching and playing with each other. These games will help them learn how to hunt later on.

A jellyfish can sense things such as light, sound and movement through its skin.

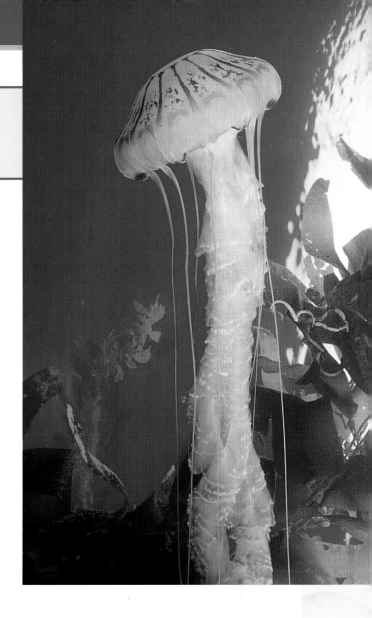

Special senses

People and animals have other special senses. These special senses work inside the body. The inside senses tell the body when it is hungry, thirsty, sleepy or in pain.

Many animals have amazing abilities that humans do not. Dogs can smell things which we cannot smell. Bats can hear things we cannot hear, which means they can hunt in the dark. Dolphins and whales can communicate over large distances in very deep water where it is too dark to see anything.

 How do birds and fish use their senses to find their way?

Birds have a sort of compass inside them which helps them to find their way around the world when they **migrate**. Some species of birds travel as much as 800 kilometres (500 miles) and back again without getting lost. Pigeons use the Sun and the stars to help them to find their way. Salmon have a special sense which helps them to find their way across oceans, back to the same river that they were born in.

 ## Exploring further – Nerves

Follow this path to discover more about the nerves that cover the human body: Contents > Digging Deeper > Thinking and feeling > The nerve network.

Green plants

Parts of plants

Plants are those living things that are not animals. Green plants include trees, bushes, grass, flowering plants, mosses, **lichens** and **algae**. The seven life processes are also necessary for plants to survive. Here we look at the life processes of green plants. Green plants need water and sunlight to grow well. Leaves, roots and stems all play a part in keeping the plant alive.

Leaves

All green plants use their leaves to make food. The leaves of green plants contain **chlorophyll**. This is what makes them green. Each leaf uses sunlight, **carbon dioxide** from the air, and water from the soil. The chlorophyll in the leaf uses the Sun's **energy** to change carbon dioxide and water into sugar and **oxygen**. This process is called **photosynthesis**.

This picture shows the main parts of a flowering plant.

• Leaves – use sunlight, carbon dioxide in the air and water to make food and **respire**.

• Flowers – contain the male and female parts of the plant needed to make seeds and **reproduce**.

• Stem – holds the plant up.

• Roots – take in water and **minerals** from the soil and hold the plant in the ground.

Mangrove trees have special roots that grow down from the trunk to give them extra stability in the swamp where they live.

Roots

The roots are the part of the plant that grow under the ground. They hold the plant in the ground. If the roots are deep it is hard to pull the plant out. Tiny hairs on the roots take in water and **nutrients** from the soil. Some plants have one big root, others have a tangled mass of roots.

Stems

The stem holds up the leaves and the flowers. A stem has many tiny tubes which carry water from the roots to the leaves. Cactus plants also store water in their fat stems.

Tree trunks are hard, woody stems. Trees need strong stems because they grow much bigger and taller than most other plants. New wood grows every year so the trunk gets thicker and stronger. Bark is hard, dead wood which protects the growing wood underneath.

Every year, trees make a new layer, or ring, of wood just below the bark. If you count the rings, you can work out how old the tree is.

Exploring further – Plant chart

Look at the chart in the Key Ideas bank on the CD-ROM. This will show you the main parts of a flowering plant and the roles they play in keeping the plant alive. Follow this path: Exploring > Green plants > How plants stay alive > Key Ideas

Flowers, fruits and seeds

Most kinds of plants produce flowers every year. Some have more than one colour. Different kinds of flowers have different shapes and numbers of **petals**, but the job of all flowers is to make seeds which will grow into new plants.

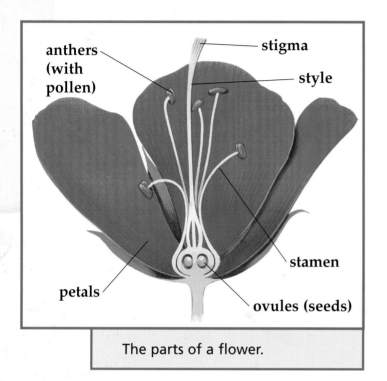

The parts of a flower.

Flowers

Flowers have both male and female parts. The male **anthers**, at the end of the **stamen**, are covered with **pollen**. In the middle of the anthers is the female **style**. The bright colours and sweet scents of flowers attract insects, which come to feed on a sweet juice called **nectar**. Some of the grains of **pollen** get stuck on each feeding insect. Some of this pollen will rub off onto the style of the next flower it visits.

Seeds

The male pollen grain lands on the **stigma** and grows down the style. Then it joins with one of the **ovules** to make a **fertilized** seed. When most of the ovules have been fertilized, the flower dies. The petals dry up and fall off, but the seeds begin to swell and ripen.

Many seeds are scattered by the wind. The seeds of some trees have wings to help them blow further.

Dandelion seeds have little parachutes which mean they can be carried great distances by the wind.

Fruits

A fruit is the part of a plant that grows around the seeds as they ripen. When the seeds are ripe, the fruits fall from the plant. If they fall on to good soil, the seeds start to grow into new plants. Some fruits, like peaches, plums and cherries have one seed in the middle of each fruit. Oranges, apples and blackberries have many seeds inside each fruit. A strawberry has many seeds too, but they are all on the outside of the fruit.

As the seeds of the apple tree ripen, the small fruits swell and grow bigger. Eventually each fruit becomes ripe.

Nuts and pods

Fruits include nuts, tomatoes and cucumbers as well as all kinds of berries. A nut is a seed with a hard shell around it. The seeds of peas, beans, lupins and many other plants grow inside pods. As the seeds swell, the pods grow longer and fatter. When the seeds are ripe, the pod splits and the seeds are thrown onto fresh ground away from the parent plant.

Exploring further – Pollen

Watch a bee gathering pollen and pollinating a flower. Follow this path on the CD-ROM: Exploring > Green plants > Pollinating flowers > Key ideas

Life cycle of a flowering plant

Sunflowers grow from large seeds. The seed is planted in the ground in spring, when the soil is warm and damp. From this seed, a sunflower plant will grow. The roots of the plant start to push down through the soil. They are covered in tiny hairs which take in water. A green **shoot** starts to grow upwards towards the surface.

After about a week the green shoot pushes through the soil. The first leaves open out. They use sunlight, air and water to make food for the plant. The plant grows taller and more leaves grow at the tip of the stem. Under the ground the roots grow longer. They take in water and the **minerals** the plant needs to stay alive. A large bud forms at the end of the stem.

Eventually the bud begins to open. Underneath are lots of yellow **petals**. The flowers open out. Hundreds of seeds will grow in the middle of the flower-head.

This sunflower is about two weeks old. It is starting to form a bud.

Each flower-head is made up of hundreds of tiny flowers called **florets**. The tips of these florets are covered with **pollen**. Honey bees see the bright yellow petals and come to the flower-head to collect pollen. As the honey bee crawls across the florets, it becomes covered with pollen. The pollen rubs off its body into the florets on other flowers and **fertilizes** them. In the centre of each floret is a tiny **ovule**. The ovule becomes a seed when the pollen joins with it.

Sunflowers turn to follow the Sun across the sky.

 What are sunflower seeds used for?

Farmers grow sunflowers for their seeds. Most of the seeds are crushed and made into animal feed or squeezed to make sunflower oil. Some seeds are roasted for us to eat as snacks. Other seeds are kept to be planted again next spring.

 ## Exploring further – Wind pollination

Some flowers are pollinated by the wind rather than by insects. Find out more about this on the CD-ROM. Follow this path: Contents > Quick Facts > Life cycles of flowers

Variation and classification

What is classification?

There are amazing numbers of living things on Earth. Each type of living thing is called a **species**. There are millions of species and scientists need a way of identifying individual ones. To do this, they divide living things into groups. This is called classification.

How does classification work?

Living things are divided into groups, depending on the features that they have in common. Here are the main groups:

- **Kingdoms** – these are the largest groups. Two main kingdoms are: the animal kingdom and the plant kingdom.
- Phyla – similar classes of living things are grouped into phyla.
- Classes – similar orders are grouped into classes.
- Orders – similar families are grouped into orders.
- Families – related genera are grouped into families.
- Genera – similar species are grouped into genera. They all have very similar features.
- Species – these are the smallest groups. Members of a species can breed together to produce young.

This is how classification works for the tiger.

Kingdom:	Animalia (animals)
Phylum:	Chordata (chordates)
Sub-phylum:	Vertebrata (**vertebrates** – have backbones)
Class:	Mammalia (mammals)
Order:	Carnivora (**carnivores**)
Family:	Felidae (cats)
Genus:	Panthera
Species:	tigris

(The **Latin** name for a tiger – *Panthera tigris* – tells us that the genus is *Panthera* and the species is *tigris*.)

Carl von Linné (1707-78)

The modern system of classification was devised by the Swedish scientist, Carl von Linné. He gave each known living thing a two-part Latin name. The huge Komodo dragon for example, is *Varanus komodoensis*. Latin was used so that the name was the same all over the world and could be understood by everyone. Von Linné even Latinized his own name to Carolus Linnaeus.

Evolution

The names of the groups helped scientists to decide what is the same and what is different about each group of living things. Living things change over millions of years. Some groups of animals disappear and others **evolve**. In 1832 Charles Darwin went to South America and the Galapagos Islands. He found that some kinds of animals had evolved differently from the same animals on different islands and the mainland. He wanted to explain why the animals became so different over time. His ideas are called the 'theory of **evolution**'.

The giant tortoises of the Galapagos Islands amazed Charles Darwin. The tortoises on each island look quite different from the tortoises on other islands in the area.

Exploring further – Darwin and evolution

Find out more about Charles Darwin and his ideas on evolution on the CD-ROM. Follow this path: Contents > Biographies

The animal kingdom

Mammals

There are more than 4000 **species** of **mammals**, ranging from huge elephants and whales to tiny bats and shrews. It is the class to which human beings also belong. Mammals are **warm-blooded vertebrates** that breathe air using lungs. They are the only animals that produce milk to feed their young. As well as **placental** mammals that give birth to live young (like humans), there are two other types of mammal.

Marsupials are mammals with pouches. They include kangaroos, koalas and wombats. Their new-born young are very tiny and weak. After birth, they crawl into their mother's pouch where they feed on milk and grow. Three species of mammal, the duck-billed platypus, the long-beaked echidna and the short-beaked echidna are monotremes, which are mammals that lay eggs.

The aardvark is the only living member of its order. This unusual ant-eating mammal lives on the grasslands of Africa. It has a long sticky tongue and strong digging claws, suitable for raiding ant-hills and termite nests.

Birds

Birds are also warm-blooded vertebrates. They are the only animals whose bodies are covered with feathers. Most birds can fly. They have beaks but no teeth. They produce their young by laying eggs with hard shells. Birds are found all over the world, in city centres, steamy **rainforests** and at the icy poles. They range in size from the huge African ostrich, which stands two metres tall, to tiny bee hummingbirds from Central America, which are no bigger than butterflies.

This hawk glides through the air on outstretched wings. The big feathers along the edge of the wing help to pull the bird through the air.

 Can all birds fly?

Some birds, such as ostriches and penguins, have wings but cannot fly. Ostriches are the largest birds in the world. They are too heavy to fly but can run at more than 70 kilometres per hour (43 miles per hour), faster than a racehorse. Penguins look clumsy on land but seem to 'fly' under water. Using its wings as flippers, the gentoo penguin can reach speeds of about 40 kilometres per hour underwater, three times faster than the fastest human swimmer.

 Exploring further – Birds

The ancestor of modern birds was Archaeopteryx, a descendant of the dinosaurs. Find out what it looked like from fossil evidence. Follow this path: Contents > Digging Deeper > Classification > Birds

Reptiles

Reptiles are **vertebrates**. Because they are **cold-blooded**, they usually live in warm places where the Sun heats their bodies up and makes them active. Although many reptiles spend a lot of time in the water, they are also **adapted** for life on land. Their scaly skin protects their bodies and stops them drying out. Most reptiles lay eggs protected by tough, leathery shells, but some give birth to live young. There are about 6500 known species of reptiles. They include snakes and lizards, alligators and crocodiles, turtles and tortoises and the tuatara.

The tuatara is the only living member of an ancient order of reptiles. Its ancestors appeared about 220 million years ago, before the first dinosaurs. Today, tuatara are only found in New Zealand. Their name comes from a local Maori word meaning 'peaks on the back', which refers to the spiky crest growing along the tuatara's back and tail.

Amphibians

Amphibians are animals that spend part of their **life cycle** in water and part on land. The ancestors of modern amphibians were the first vertebrates to leave the water to search for food and to live on land about 370 million years ago. Amphibians are cold-blooded vertebrates. They have smooth, scaleless skin. Frogs and toads are amphibians. Amphibians spend their adult lives on land but they must return to the water to breed and lay their eggs.

Newts and salamanders are amphibians. This is a fire salamander.

Fish

There are as many **species** of fish as all other vertebrates (amphibians, reptiles, birds and mammals) put together. Fish are cold-blooded. They live in water, both fresh and salty, and 'breathe' in **oxygen** through gills. Fish are designed for swimming. They have muscular, streamlined bodies often covered in scales, and fins instead of limbs.

Invertebrates

Invertebrates are animals that do not have **vertebrae** (backbones) inside their bodies. With some 950,000 species, there are far more invertebrates than vertebrates on Earth. About 97 per cent of animal species are invertebrates. They are divided into many different groups, including insects, molluscs, worms, starfish and jellyfish.

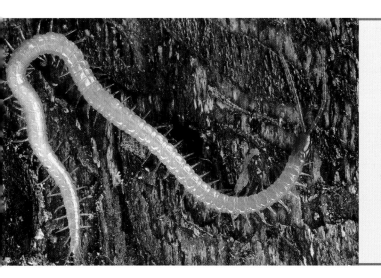

The biggest group of invertebrates is the **arthropods**. With over a million known species, it is the largest group of animals on Earth. This centipede is a member of this group.

Exploring further – Micro-organisms

Micro-organisms are living organisms that are often too small to be seen. Learn about their good and bad points on the CD-ROM. Follow this path:
Explore > Living Things and Their Environments > Micro-organisms

The plant kingdom

The plant **kingdom** is divided into flowering plants and those that do not produce flowers. Plants without flowers have been growing on Earth for 300 million years.

Non-flowering plants

Most non-flowering plants grow from tiny, dust-like specks called **spores**. The spores are released in their thousands, and carried away by the wind. If they land in a suitable place, they grow into new plants.

Algae are very simple, non-flowering plants, with no proper roots, leaves or stems. They usually grow in water and range in size from microscopic, single-**celled** plants to gigantic seaweeds.

Mosses and liverworts are mainly small, ground-hugging plants that live in damp places. They do not have flowers but produce their spores in a small capsule that is held up on a tiny stalk. When the capsule opens, the spores are carried away on the wind.

Ferns, horsetails and clubmosses also grow from spores. You can see the spores on the underside of the leaves on this fern.

Are trees flowering or non-flowering plants?

There are two common groups of trees: **conifers** and broad-leaved trees. Conifers are non-flowering and broad-leafed trees are flowering plants. Conifers are trees such as pines, larches and redwoods. There are about 550 species of conifers and their **pollen**, **ovules** and seeds grow in woody cones. Most broad-leaved trees are **deciduous**. This means that they lose their leaves once a year.

A field of poppies. Poppies are dicotyledons.

Flowering plants

Flowering plants are by far the biggest group of plants with about 250,000 species. They first grew on Earth about a hundred million years ago. Flowering plants can be divided into two classes: monocotyledons and dicotyledons. A cotyledon is a tiny leaf inside a seed. Until the new plant grows its first leaves, it lives off food stored in the cotyledon. Monocotyledons have only one of these leaves in their seeds. Dicotyledons have two cotyledons in their seeds.

Exploring further – Using plants

We use plants not only for food, but for construction, clothing, paper and medicines. Follow this path on the CD-ROM to find out how: Contents > Digging Deeper > Plants > Plants and Us

Living things in their environment

Habitats

The place where plants and animals live is called a **habitat**. Habitats can be mountains, lakes, woods, oceans and seashores. Some animals can survive in many kinds of habitat. Certain species of birds can do this. But most living things occupy just one kind of habitat. Some would not be able to live anywhere else.

There are many kinds of habitats. Woods, fields, moors, lakes, rivers and sandy shores are quite large habitats. A hedge, a back garden and a rock pool are smaller habitats. A habitat can be as small as the space under a stone or a single leaf of a plant.

Plants need light, water, warmth and **nutrients** to grow. Each habitat has its good and bad points. Woods are fairly damp, dark and shady habitats. Fields get plenty of light but are often drier than woods. Mountain tops are much colder than sheltered valleys. Some soils have more nutrients than others.

A pond is a habitat. Many kinds of plants and animals live there, including reeds, insects, fish and birds.

The desert is a very harsh habitat, but some plants such as cacti are able to live there. This cactus has a thick fleshy stem which helps it retain water.

Different plants and animals do well in different habitats. Moss is a plant which grows better in damp, shady places than in dry, sunny places. So you are more likely to find moss in a wood than on a sunny window-ledge.

Preserving habitats

Changing or damaging a habitat affects the living things that live there. For example, when a tree is cut down, all the insects, birds and other animals that lived there lose their habitat. They must find a new place to live or they will die. The plants and animals that lived in the shade under the tree also have their habitat changed. An oak tree may have 400 different kinds of animals living in or under it. They include insects, spiders, worms, mice, birds and squirrels. Thousands of living things are affected when an oak tree is cut down.

Exploring further – Animals in danger

The CD-ROM can tell you why some animals are in danger due to loss of their habitats. Follow this path: Contents > Digging Deeper > Animals in Danger

Adaptation

The living world is packed with incredible variety and diversity. Living things vary from tiny **micro-organisms** to massive whales and giant trees. Each living thing has features that allow it to survive in its **habitat**. These features are known as adaptations. Each living thing is suited, or **adapted**, to its habitat.

A wide variety of habitats

The world has many different types of habitats, such as mountains, lakes, woods and seashores. Most living things are adapted to one particular habitat. This is so common and natural that we rarely notice it. A dolphin could not live on land; it could not move or feed out of water. A camel could not survive in the open sea; it would very quickly drown. Neither type of animal is adapted to the other's habitat.

Sea anemones are adapted to living in the **tidal** zone on the seashore. When the tide is high, they extend their tentacles to catch prey, then as the tide falls they close up like blobs of jelly.

Camels are adapted to life in the hot, dry desert. Their bodies are good at retaining water and they have large feet to stop them sinking into soft sand.

Needs for survival

All living things have certain needs or requirements from their habitat, if they are to survive. These include food, **oxygen**, water, shelter and protection and a **mate** for breeding.

 How do habitats change?

Conditions in a habitat are always changing. The **seasons** and weather bring changes such as rain, storms, **droughts**, frost and snow. On the seashore the tides rise and fall. These are natural changes and animals have adapted to cope with them. Not all changes are natural. People have changed many **environments** by cutting down trees, turning land into farmland and building towns and cities. If living things are to survive, they must also be able cope with these changing conditions by adapting to them.

Many animals, especially those that **scavenge** in their natural habitats like gulls, fit in well in **urban** habitats. The rubbish tip is like a vast supermarket for them, full of all kinds of wonderful foods.

 ## Exploring further – Rainforests

Find out about the animals that are adapted to life in a **rainforest**. Follow this path on the CD-ROM: Contents > Digging Deeper > Up a rainforest tree

Interdependence

Food chains

The living things in a **community** are linked together by what they eat. For example, plants are eaten by snails, which in turn may be eaten by birds. In this way, the energy produced by green plants is passed along the **food chain**.

In the Arctic a food chain might look like this:

| fish eat sea plants | → | seals eat the fish | → | polar bears eat the seals |

Plants

Plants capture the Sun's light energy and use it to produce new growth, so they are called **producers**. Animals eat plants and other animals so they are called **consumers**. Plants start off every food chain. All animals, including human beings, ultimately rely on plants for their food.

Herbivores

The animals in the next link in the food chain are animals that live entirely on plants. They are called **herbivores** or **primary consumers**. They range from tiny insects that suck plant juices to huge elephants that uproot whole trees. Because their plant food is often not very nutritious, they have to spend a large part of their lives eating in order to get enough energy.
On the African grasslands, animals such as giraffes and elephants eat the leaves from trees and bushes. They are called **browsers**. Other animals, such as zebras and antelopes, eat grass. They are called **grazers**.

Zebras are grazers. They live on the wide African savannah.

Carnivores

Meat-eating animals are called **carnivores**. They are the next link in the food chain. Carnivores are **predators** – animals that hunt other animals (their **prey**) to eat. They have special features for hunting and eating their prey. These may include sharp, pointed teeth and claws for gripping and tearing prey. Finding food can take a great deal of time and energy. There may be more than one carnivore in the food chain. A large carnivore, such as a lion, is not eaten by any other animal and so is at the top of the food chain.

Wolves are typical carnivores. They have large, dagger-like front teeth, called canines, for gripping prey. They hunt in well-organized packs.

Omnivores

Omnivores are animals that can feed on both plants and meat. They include bears, rats, pigs, chimpanzees and human beings. Because omnivores feed on a wide variety of foods, they usually have no problem finding enough to eat. Omnivores may appear at several stages in the food chain.

Exploring further – Food chains

Look in the Key Ideas bank to see food chains in a forest, grassland, pond and in the sea. Follow this path: Contents > Key Ideas > Food Chains

What do scientists do?

Scientists want to know more about the world and how to look after it. They ask questions about all the things in our world that affect how we live, how comfortable we are and how we keep healthy. For hundreds of years, scientists have studied plants, animals and materials and tried to find out why certain things happen.

We all need to understand about science and how a scientist works. To become a good scientist you will need to be curious about the things you use, the things you see and the things that happen around you.

Part of being a scientist is asking questions. Some of these questions can be answered by reading books and using CD-ROMs and the Internet.

Sometimes you will want to find out the answer by doing a scientific investigation. You will need to collect information and use this to try to give an answer to your question. Sometimes our questions are not answered and we need to try again with a different investigation.

Once you have collected your information, you need to record it. Then you will need to think about what your results mean and what you can learn from them.

Doing all these things can help you to learn more about the world. When you can understand how important it is to carry out the scientific process correctly, then you will be well on your way to becoming a good scientist.

Exploring further

There are many ways in which you can contribute to the conservation of wildlife and the preservation of the planet. The Heineman Explore CD-ROM can give you advice on how to do this and the associated web site, **www.explorescience.com** will give you many further areas to explore.

Weblinks

You can find out more about this area of science by looking at the Weblinks on the CD-ROM. Here is a selection of sites available:

www.wwf.org
The WWF is the world's largest independent conservation organization. The WWF conserves wildlife and the natural environment for present and future generations.

4learning.co.uk/weblogic/essentials/science/life/index.jsp
Channel 4's learning site tells you all about life processes. Check out the image bank for amazing photos of bacteria, duck-billed platypuses and a very greedy Venus fly-trap!

www.bbc.co.uk/nature/
The BBC's animals site. Go to the Really Wild Zone for information on all sorts of animals, including fun activities, the latest news, and links to programmes.

www.enchantedlearning.com/subjects/rainforest/
Learn all about rainforests and the creatures that live in them. In what ways are rainforests, and the plants that live in them, important to humans?

www.bornfree.org.uk
Virginia McKenna's site has the latest information on campaigns to save gorillas, tigers and other animals.

Further reading

Super Science Book of Life Processes, David Glover, Wayland: 1994
Classification, Holly Wallace, Heinemann Library, Oxford: 2000
Life Cycles, Holly Wallace, Heinemann Library, Oxford: 2000
Food Chains and Webs, Holly Wallace, Heinemann Library, Oxford: 2000
Survival and Change, Steve Parker, Heinemann Library, Oxford: 2000
Adaptation, Steve Parker, Heinemann Library, Oxford: 2000
Life Cycle of a Guinea Pig, Angela Royston, Heinemann London: 1998

Glossary

adapt/adaptation when an animal or plant changes its features over many generations to survive in its habitat

algae simple plant-like organisms found in water and on the branches and trunks of trees – includes seaweeds

amphibians animals such as frogs, toads and newts that live both in and out of water

anthers part of a flower that contains the pollen

arthropod invertebrate with jointed limbs and a hard exoskeleton – includes insects and spiders

biceps muscles in the top part of your arm

brood young of animals, especially birds

browsers animals that eat the leaves of trees or bushes

carbon dioxide gas found in the air. Plants use it when making food and animals give it off when they breathe.

carnivore animal that only eats other animals

cartilage firm white substance, not quite as hard as bone

cell the building blocks of all living things. Each part of your body consists of millions of microscopic cells. Each kind of cell is different and does a particular job.

chlorophyll green colouring found in plant cells. It helps the plant to make its own food.

cold-blooded animals that cannot control the temperature of their bodies. They rely on the weather to warm them up or cool them down. They need to be warm to move about and search for food.

community plants and animals that live in a certain habitat

conifer trees like pine trees that produce cones

consumers animals that feed directly on plants, or indirectly by eating other animals

deciduous trees and plants that regularly shed their leaves

down soft, fluffy feathers on a bird

drought long period without rain

embryo a developing baby from the first division of cells until all the main structures have formed. In humans this is 8 weeks after conception.

energy power that living things need to keep working properly

environment surroundings that make up the place where you live

evolve/evolution how living things change and adapt over time to be better suited to surviving in their habitat

excretion getting rid of waste matter

exoskeletons tough, outer coat or shell of invertebrates such as insects or crabs. It protects and supports their soft bodies.

fertilization/fertilized when a male sex cell joins a female sex cell to make a new cell. The new cell grows into a new living thing

fibre bulky food with texture

floret a tiny flower, which is part of a flower-head

food chain natural system in which smaller animals get eaten by bigger animals, who get eaten by even bigger animals

fungi living things such as mushrooms, toadstools and moulds. Fungi are not animals or plants.

grazers animals that eat or graze on grass

habitat a particular place where plants and animals live

herbivore animal that eats only vegetable matter

incubate keep eggs warm so that they hatch

invertebrate animal that does not have a backbone inside its body

kingdom in scientific classification, the largest group of living things. There are five kingdoms including plants, animals and fungi.

Latin language from ancient Rome

lichen light-green plant that grows on rocks or trees

life cycle stages of development in a living organism from the very earliest moments until it is able to reproduce

mammals warm-blooded animals, like humans, that feed their young on their mother's milk

marsupial mammal that has a pouch in which its baby grows

mate 1. when a male and female come together to make babies. 2. partner of an animal

micro-organism living thing that is so tiny it can only be seen through a microscope

migrate/migration when animals travel long distances to move to a better place to find food and shelter or mate

mineral simple substance that is found naturally in the Earth. They can help to build your body and keep it healthy.

nectar sweet, sugary liquid made inside a flower. Bees and butterflies visit a flower to drink the nectar. While they are drinking, their bodies get covered in pollen for pollination.

nerve cord that sends messages between a part of the body and the brain

nutrients the parts of food which the body needs for energy or to build new cells

nutrition how living things take in and digest food

omnivore animal that eats both plants and animals

organs internal parts of the body that perform particular functions

ovule female part of a plant which turns into a seed after fertilization

oxygen gas in the air. Living things need to breathe in oxygen to stay alive.

parasite animal that lives off the body of another animal

petal delicate parts around the outside of a flower. They are usually brightly coloured and are often scented to attract insects.

photosynthesis the way green plants make food from sunlight, carbon dioxide and water

placental placental mammals are those whose young develop inside their mother's bodies until they are fully formed

pollen tiny grains of powder that are the special male parts of a plant

predators animals that hunt and kill other animals for food

prey animals that are hunted and killed for food

primary consumer animal that feeds directly on plants. The word primary means 'first'.

producer green plants that produce or make their own food. They start off nearly every food chain.

protein substance found in some foods which living things need to grow new cells and replace old ones

rainforest rainy place where many trees and plants grow together

receptor organ that is adapted to receive information

reproduce/reproduction to have children or young; to make new life

reptiles animals with scaly skin that breathe in air. They include snakes, lizards and turtles. Dinosaurs were reptiles.

respire/respiration how living things take in and use oxygen

retina sensitive layer at the back of the eye

scavenge/scavenger to feed on refuse and dead animals

seasons parts of the year that have different weather (like summer and winter)

sensitivity how sensitive something is

shoot first stem and leaves of a new plant

species group of living things that have certain features in common and in which the male and female can breed together

spore tiny speck of living material. Some plants, like mushrooms, grow from spores.

stamen male reproductive organ of a plant

starch sugars in food

stigma part of a flower that receives the pollen

style part of a flower that bears the stigma

teats part of a mammal that feeds its babies with milk

tendon part of the body that joins muscles to bones

tidal rise and fall of the surface of the sea

triceps muscles in your upper arm. They pull to straighten your arm.

urban to do with towns and cities

vertebrae the individual bones which make up the spine, or backbone

vertebrate animal with a backbone inside its body

vitamins chemicals that the body needs to stay healthy

warm-blooded animal that can control its own body temperature. This means it can live in hot and cold places and still stay active and alert.

water vapour water in gas form

Index